REFLECTIONS OF A SHATTERED MIND

Reflections of a Shattered Mind

of a

ANTHONY MARCUCIO

CONNECTICUT • 2021

Illustrations by Diana Rose Smith

Author Photo by Bonnie Hakins of Bon-Bon's Photography

Book Design by Words by Jen (Branford, CT)

ISBN 978-0-578-75602-8

Printed in the U.S.A.

Introduction

Depression and anxiety are mental health conditions that affect millions of lives, both directly and indirectly. They have been a part of my life for as long as I can remember. Though I have tried different treatments and coping methods through the years, poetry has always been the constant that has helped me through my darkest times and allowed me to tell my story. Being male, it was always difficult to discuss due to the stigma surrounding mental health. In recent years, I was finally able to find the courage to speak up. These poems are a gateway through my journey with mental health. They travel through my highest highs, my lowest lows, and everything in between. My hope is that my story will encourage others to stand up to help fight the stigma we face with mental health.

Contents

"Faith is the strength by which a shattered world shall emerge into the light."

— Helen Keller

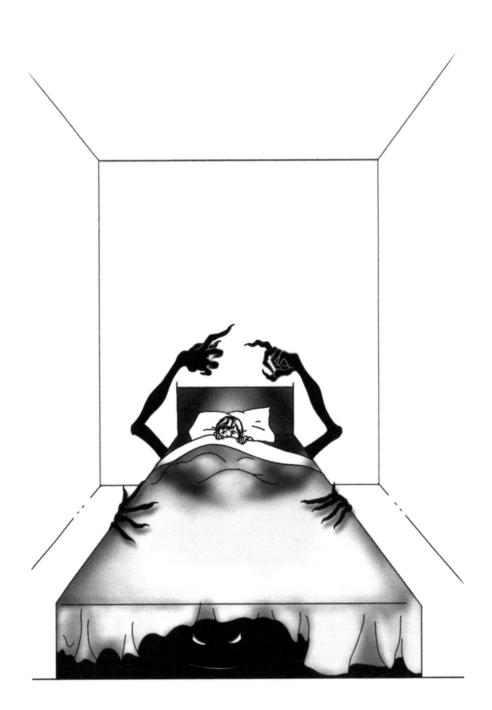

Cleanse My Sins

Is the monster in the closet
Or is he under my bed
Is he scheming with the demons
Who live inside my head

Praying for a moment of peace
Begging to be exorcised
Dousing me in holy water
To cleanse my sins and lies

But drowning in my tears
There's forever no release
Caressing each and every fear
Taunting is the beast

Hoping for my thirst to quench
I am drinking this red rum
The clouded night is endless
There's no more rising sun

Chain me to the bed
As the darkness isolates
Demons, I do implore you
For my mind to immolate

Society's bladed edge
Piercing deeper in my soul
Medicating fallacies
As I slowly lose control

The monster holds my right arm
The demon binds my left
The beast pulls the strings
My vitality escapes my breath

Lying motionless on the floor
The claws have scarred my arm
Though lifeless as I remain
I'm finally free from harm

The Mask

This mask is suffocating
Staring in the mirror
So unremarkable the disguise
It is real to the touch
Yes, conceal the agony
There is nothing left to feel
But you still do
The mask is perfect
The whole world fooled
The deception is perfect
Just keep smiling
An exhausting costume to wear
My knees bleed from praying
Maybe one day I can see
Maybe one day I can unmask
Can it be normal?
Can I be normal?
Maybe one day
But for now, the mask remains

Battlefield of Lies

There is struggle within my eyes
My mind is a battlefield of lies
Echoing are my silent cries
All these fallacies I despise
Know my heart has so tried
Hiding behind forged pride
Committing emotional suicide
Can you answer my questions why
I have more lows than I do highs
As I grasp up to the sky
Beseech my soul not to die

Jericho

I'm trapped in Jericho
The truth behind the walls
Clandestine reality
Imploring them to fall

Disguised on the surface
Keeping invasion at bay
The proverbs revealed
No relief from the fray

Help liberate my soul
The walls are closing in
Solidity is crumbling
Devoured by my sins

Sleep Paralysis

I am paralyzed
I try to scream
But I can't
I feel the demon
He is staring at me
He is scaring me
I assure you
I am awake
I can only lie and wait
Silently screaming
Struggling to move
Waiting for the moment
For all of this to end
So I can breathe again

Dreams of Foolish Light

What causes me to chase
These dreams of foolish light
Which truth do I seek
Suppressing inner strife

Am I blind to scripture
What is it that I see
Grasping at the straws
Of a hoaxed reality

What pushes me further
Toward these counterfeit scenes
When anguish pulls me deeper
With these distorted dreams

Medusa's Delight

Your laughter alluring
Seducing life's fate
Man shows sinful might
Guiding him blindly
Mesmerized by dance
Your hair hisses delight
The foolish chase greed
As they gaze into your eyes
Turned to stone with your sight

My Workday with Depression

Came in to work today
Trying to hide my fears
Trying to fight my tears
Careful of what I say

Have a meeting at ten
Just need to get through this
My heart just feels like Swiss
Can't wait for this to end

This is not what I hoped
The meeting is delayed
My fear is not portrayed
More time for me to cope

Just want to be alone
Then I can breathe and sigh
Or maybe just to cry
Be in my quiet zone

I just hate days like this
Trapped in reality
These visions you can't see
Just more pain to resist

No End in Time

These primal terrors shatter my mind
The horrors I see show no end in time
The visions inside are not sublime

I see the angels calling for rapture
My soul is left for them to capture
But I can feel my will fracture

My pain has taught me to despise
No shelter hides me from the lies
Abandoned still with silent cries

She Stayed on the Moon

She said she loved me to the moon and back
But when my love went to the moon, she stayed
The man on the moon had worked his magic
Before I knew it, he swept her away

Tinnitus

I wish I could stop this
Ringing cursing my head
I crave the silence
I yearn for peace
I can't remember
Times of quiet nights
Some days I fly through
No struggle on my mind
But when I need tranquility
There is just ringing
No end in sight
Echoing through my mind
Struggling to hear
Just the simple sounds
Sometimes I pray
But there is still ringing

Truthful Lies

In my mind I see my purifying sins
I see my demons are exonerated
They are telling me their truthful lies
The serpent is counting these wins
All these fallacies are celebrated
I can feel the suicidal soul's cries

Maybe One Day

Maybe one day I will know normal
Maybe they will invent a switch
Perhaps a button on the brain
So when my hours are darkest
I can just turn it off and feel peace
Imagine that!
Just a switch to dull the pain
Or maybe a reset
But there are so many questions!
How will I feel?
Peaceful
Numb
Relieved
How will I change?
Will I lose my empathy?
Will I remember my pain?
Oh, but there is so much curiosity!
It makes me wonder
What does ignorance feel like?
Is it truly blissful?
Maybe one day I can forget
So this pain isn't a constant reminder
Maybe one day I can turn it off
Maybe one day I will hear silence
Imagine the joy without a thousand thoughts at once
Maybe one day I can feel peace

Reflections of a Shattered Mind

I see the shattered glass
Lying on the ground
Broken memories abound
Reflecting with no sound

Can I sweep the shards
Will I feel it drain
Cutting through my pain
Show me what remains

What is this memory
I'm staring in my eyes
Is this truth or lies
Tell me what I despise

Muddled as I see
Show me my reflection
Through my mind's dissection
Where is my redemption

Please show me clarity
What am I to do
Please tell me what is true
My last memory is of you

Voice inside Your Head

Do you hear me today?
Do you know what I say?
My words can guide your way

I'm the voice inside your head
With all the words I said
I fill your thoughts with dread

All these doubts of reality
Pondering all that you see
The devil tips his hat to me

Why do your friends remain?
Is this all in vain?
Are you sure you are sane?

Silence is what hurts most
Haunted by all these ghosts
From pasts we have not spoke

I have you convinced of lies
With truths you do despise
And all your feeble alibis

I come when you're in pain
Your darkest hour is profane
How do you still remain?

My words will not be silent
The memories become violent
Corrupting you like a tyrant

I feed off fear and ire
Struggle fuels my desire
My words will not retire

I fill your thoughts with dread
With all the words I said
I'm the voice inside your head

What Happened to My Tears

Pain runs through me
Is it poison to give me death?
Is it someone stopping my breath?
It feels like death is calling me
Tears stop falling
But the pain is still there
It's something I wish not to share
No more will I fear
I want no more tears
Let me swallow my cares
The pain drives me to my knees
Brings me where I wish not to be
I close my eyes just to see
Can you tell me where I stand?
Inside is cold and dark
I see no flicker or a spark
Did my soul release and depart?
What happened to my tears?
I feel so numb and still
Movements inside seem unreal
I lay in bed as I hope to heal
My strength is stolen
I can stand but am weak
I hear the whispers sound so meek
In my mind is truth I seek

Blackened Skies

Blackened skies fill my head
My heart is pure
But my soul is dead

Slipping through my hands
Like the sands of time
Mind traveling through lands

Acceptance of anger and fear
What thought impossibility
Now brings a tear

Shadows seem real
Pain ever-present
Is my fate sealed?

Hoping for a sign
Knees praying deeply
For the past pine

Eyes masked wet
Beyond lonely hope
The sun will not set

Darkness within a Broken Soul

Raptures of the wicked
Describing scenes of terror
No response is returned
By the man in the mirror

Black Sunday shines upon
The grave of a broken soul
Set forth in motion the wheels
Turning from the times of old

The sins, the lies, the horror within
Even true forms take great disguise
When corrupted by lost youth
Bring many chambers inside

Chains binding the hero
With sweet sympathy to his death
The devil's brew takes control
Binding every thought and breath

Within the forgotten realms
The lonely bard cries
For the demons possess the soul
Hidden beneath the lies

Do You See the Signs?

Forsaking my words
Condemned by society
Judging by the cover
Ignoring what is reality

A cry for help
My hand is reaching
But blind by falsehoods
All I hear is preaching

Troubled is the soul
Fighting all this pain
But pressure from our peers
Makes a man insane

Fearing all the worst
From all the words you see
Twisting pure innocence
From fake reality

Do you see the signs
In front of you they lay
Struggling to cope
What words can you say

Do you see me reaching
For simple sympathy
Praying that you notice
My need for empathy

Or will time tick down
Reaching out my hand
Slowly passing through
Just like grains of sand

Shadows of the Past

Menacing cries
From lies of the past
Awaiting the moment
Of the soul's final grasp

Away in the silence
The warrior fell
And made but a sound
With his shattered shell

The sands of time
Slip slowly away
His soul hollowed
By its nomadic sway

Twin gems shine dim
With empty stares to the void
The demon's brew pursued
With the shadows deployed

The whispering wind
Calls his name true
Seeing through the looking glass
Of a past he once knew

The storm brews high
Within the wicked realm
Slowly withering away
Beneath the lonely elm

Left Behind

The siren's song
Is all but passed
Echoing silently
In the halls of the past

Cupid is gone
His arrow flew by
Love lost within
The reaches of the sky

Still waters
Hold shallow sympathy
For along the rolling plains
Runs a deep apathy

Nevermore

Watching...
Wishing...
Waiting...
Yet the response
Seems many miles away
From an angel so pure
Truth is masked
By the deceit
Of a fallen soul
As the requite
Holds false hope
Nevermore shall thy soul rest...

Revelations of Society

Not a kid anymore
Days keep passing by
Reading the scriptures
The book of Revelations
Has me seeing through mind's eye

Sharp as an arrow
Armageddon is coming
I see it in my dreams
The child is crying
You see the fear running

Dark angels surrounding
Swallowing innocent souls
But Lucifer's work
Is not in the midst
But society's lack of control

What is it I see
As I gently lay my head
I close my eyes...
I dream...
Give no words to be said

A Masked Reality

Assumptions seem true
Of a corrupted past
Innocence lost with age
Within a masked reality
Encrypting beliefs of life
Is the work of the dark mage

Through the sands of time
Life's promise drifts away
Upon different roads of life
Hidden truth lies within
Deep in eyes of purity
Falling to painful strife

Truth within the Soul

The sirens sing
A song of silence
Echoing through the hills
As I remove
A mystical dagger
From my heart

Fooled twice
By lies and deceit
What a shame
To live your life
Past, present, and future
In a bed of fallacy

Truth once seemed
Such a strong gesture
But by night
Has faded along
The desolate void
Of the dark pasture

Conceiving of evils, no true friend
Can withstand the lure
Of the serpent's lair
The muse of the underworld
Takes heed approaching
The chamber of darkness

The soul sits quietly
Watching...
Wishing...
Waiting...
For truth to surface
But it is lost in the abyss...

Unseen

Don't be deceived
By these blue eyes
Hiding all
Pain and lies
Learning faith
To despise
To my knees
I have tried
Emotional music
Of suicide
Can you hear
The silent cries
With walls closing
On all sides
Leave me still
As I lie
Decay unseen
As my soul dies

Spiraling into Insanity

Are these lies or reality
I fear my own mentality
Spiraling into insanity
Trials only the blind can see

Demons won't go away
Mind left with nomadic sway
Will you go or stay
Speak the words I cannot say

Spinning wheel round and round
Allow my mind homeward bound
Plant my feet on the ground
Leave my soul without a sound

The Devil Walks among Us

The devil walks among us
Through the city streets
Hiding in plain sight
With everyone he meets

He sees inside your soul
You cannot hide your fears
Has always been the same
Through many, many years

The devil walks among us
Claiming all tragedies
From the highest mountain top
To the deepest seas

From the snake in the garden
To every ounce of pain
Making deals for your soul
Until no more remain

The devil walks among us
Invading all your dreams
Distorting your reality
Nothing is what it seems

Do you see the sin of man
Spreading like a cancer
Disasters big and small
Still searching for the answers

The devil walks among us
We are terrorized by war
Or maybe it is sweet revenge
Hoping to settle the score

Guns and money all abound
Lust and greed and lies
He can see right through your mask
And your feeble alibis

The devil walks among us
Bringing many lives to Hell
Tempting with the apple
And all he has to sell

Those who struggle quiet
Suffer most of all
Casualties of society
Forgotten as they fall

The devil walks among us
Leaving horror in his wake
His wicked smile flashing bright
Pleasures for his own sake

Do you see all the pain
It comes in bounds and leaps
Reality brings foolish pride
As society still weeps

The Reflection of Your Eyes

The reflection
When I look
Deep into your eyes
A gift truly
Yet...
The words do not
Hold a volume
When I see you
Told once of true love
Holding sacred
What seems to be
Lies of consequence
Save tonight
For what I see
Your image
Etched into my mind
A face
Yet...
No touch...
No caress...
Just simplicity
Of no such love
For the only lasting memory
Is the reflection
Of your eyes

I Know

Why you can't sleep
Why the blade cuts deep
Why you hide in fear
Why you feel no care
Why at night you cry
Why you want to die
Why you will not speak
Inside there is truth you seek
Why you are in pain
The struggle to remain sane
How fast the mind spins
Why these feel like sins
Some days you wish to end
But know I am here for you, my friend
Your strength will let you see
How you can again feel free

Man Up

Man up
Be a man
Real men don't cry
That's not manly
You're too sensitive
Stop being a baby
Get over it

So here I sit
Alone in my corner
Fighting these tears
Suppressing these fears
So, I stand
I take a deep breath
Because I need to man up

Hook the Hero

What if Captain Hook
Was really just the hero
And we were deceived?

Fallen Angel, Allow Me Sight

Within the wicked realms
The fiery demon lies
The bloody soul of a child
Is corrupted through despise

Sweet angel from above
Tell me the reasons why
So many times I was shadowed
But now I see you cry

Your wings have departed
No more do you fly
I just watch and wonder
As you fall from the sky

Are my sins so great
They bring tears to your eyes
No more will you mask me
From fate's vexing lies

Conceiving of this evil
For you, my soul cries
Fallen angel from above
This scene I can't deny

Seeing you helpless
Struggling to survive
My heart does weep
From the pain in your eyes

No more can you save me
Goodness passes by
Your lonely body diminished
Asking questions why

Don't shed your tears
My soul does try
The time has come
To say goodbye

Allow me to see
Through my own eyes
Allow me the pleasure
Of society's lies

Wipe that tear
From your eye
Tend to your wings
Again shall you fly

Allow me freedom
I will be wise
Mistakes will be made
But my soul will not lie

I can see now
As blood stains my eyes
The world is crumbling
Through all of its lies

Don't cry for me now
I still see the sun rise
Smile down upon me
My soul will never die

Lightning Storm

I watch the lightning flash
Lighting up the sky
Flickering on and off
As it catches my eye

I hear the thunder rumble
Shaking the earth below
Sometimes it crashes loud
Others it stays low

The rain dances in the light
Cleansing all around
With peace and tranquility
Spreads a calming sound

Raise Me Up

Be my voice
when I can't speak
Be my strength
when I am weak

Guide me through
when I wander
Sharpen my mind
If I do ponder

Calm my fears
When I'm beset
Show a path
With no regret

Cleanse my soul
When I sin
Allow me to search
Deep within

Pray for me
When faith is shaken
Raise me up
When my time is taken

Sing the Song of Bards

Sing the song of bards
Bring courage to thy man
Sing for all the children
And the women across the land

Sing the song of bards
Of past heroes oh so great
Sing to stir the gods above
Where angels learn their fate

Sing the song of bards
So faithful and so true
Sing a song so purely
It can only be sung by you

Sing the song of bards
Let the people be inspired
Allow the notes to carry
All throughout the shire

Sing the song of bards
Sing to bring such joy
To all the men and women
And every girl and boy

Sing the song of bards
Tell tales of the past
Sing a song so pure in soul
In hearts it shall last

Starless Night

Starless night
How can you see?
Where are your eyes
To look down upon me?

Save me from
The evil's brew
Unmask the shadows
Bring life anew

If you cry
Don't hide your tears
Let my gaze
Ease your fears

Show me life
Starless night
Brighten my path
Give me light

Lead me through
The depths unknown
A friend in need
Where courage is grown

Starless night
Lead me through
The peaceful sky
To be with you

Sweet Child, Smile for Me

I know it's hard sometimes
Just to put on a smile
There's heartache and pain
It gets lonely all the while

But there is a calm within
The eye of every storm
And there's always a heart
To keep you warm

Remember, sweet child
There is always greener grass
Just search within the pasture
Through your looking glass

Sweet child today
Smile for me
It'll ease my fears
And calm the seas

Your smile is so bright
It illuminates the sky
The breeze caresses your face
With no questions why

Keep true in your heart
Don't stray from the path
Push aside your worries
Of society's harsh wrath

Let people see
Your beautiful eyes
Let people see
Your strength inside

Search for the stars
In the sky above
Allow your heart freedom
To see that peaceful dove

Your smile warms my heart
Don't let your soul fade
Allow the peace to fill within
And guide you through the day

No More

No more will I hide in fear
No more will I shed tears
No more will you tear me down
No more will I wear this frown
No more love is left inside
My passion within has surely died
No more will I chase a dream
My eyes have opened to what's unseen
Know that I am all cried out
No longer do I hold any doubt
For so long I thought it was me
Something inside I could not see
No more lonely nights asleep
No more praying for you to keep
No more depriving intimacy
No more do I wander blindly
I have tried and tried for so long
Today I am finally gone

My Story Still Untold

I can feel the weight
Of my dreams being crushed
With the slightest of gasps
Leaving my words hushed

With tragedy so pure
What is there to do
Rise up and press on
This, I implore you

Simple seeds within
Shining through the cracks
Picking up the pieces
From society's attacks

But as I move forward
My story still untold
Gathering strength again
These images are bold

To hear my words echo
Holding truthful reasons
I continue to fight
For you through the seasons

Toxicity in Your Masculinity

Do you see the toxicity
Hiding in your masculinity
Acting like you're divinity
A part of the Holy Trinity
So clear the blind can see
No ways to be set free
Trapped in your fragility
Say the words you can't speak to me
Will your eyes open and see
Your actions that should not be
Hiding in your family tree
Keep your words away from me
Values that you can't foresee
The foolishness you guarantee
My friend, this is not manly
Blind in your actuality
Open up and you will see
Leave your fear behind door three
Don't be scared of the key
Unlocking truth to feel so free
Knowing real masculinity
Has no place for toxicity

Journey above the Clouds

When I walk in the woods
Nature tells me a tale
My imagination runs wild
Allowing my mind to set sail

Such a symphony
With oh so many sounds
My senses are in heaven
With sights and scents abound

Imagine if you will
Taking flight with a bee
Buzzing with the breeze
Would be such a sight to see

But now is the bee too small
To take on such a journey
I want to soar much higher
To quench my growing yearning

A bird will suit much better
But where do I begin?
Do I take the finch or cardinal
Maybe a blue jay or robin

But now upon their feathers
We can glide above the trees
Basking in the brightest sun
And gliding through the breeze

Now this is such a sight
All the lakes and mountain tops
The smells and sounds and colors
I hope it never stops

But is this all I can see
Surely there is more
Maybe I can climb on a goose
To see how far he'll soar

Imagine so many more
Sights along the coast
The wonders through this trip
I ask what I need most

I open my eyes as I see
My feet again on the ground
Taking in the scene around me
With each and every sound

Maybe I was blinded
Where everything I seek
Surrounded me this whole time
With all the world I need

The Rose

I see the rose before me
Climbing upon the leaves
The thorns are sharp
I climb the stalk to the petals
Seeing all the beauty
Gazing upon the top of the rose
I see all sorts of blooms
Marigolds and petunias
Lilies and sunflowers
Sounds of bees buzzing
The chirping of the birds
A soothing melody to my ears
The tranquility on these soft petals
Is this Utopia?
But slowly they float to the ground
One by one, from the cold breeze
Chill replaces the warmth
No more songs are sung
I see the rose in pain
Beauty still shows
But the vision is false
The petals can't hold my weight
I'm falling
I try to hold on to the stem
The thorns cut deep
The pain is too great
My decent hastens
So sudden a change!

The warm sun is gone
Cold and gray I see before me
I've fallen to the ground
Solid as a rock
My body is torn
My hands are bleeding
I look up to the rose
No petals
No leaves
Imperfections remain
My blood drips from the thorns
I see the pain on the rose
This image remains
Dark and gray
Cold and empty
But temporary is the pain
Soon the sun will shine
Soon the sky will warm
I will see the rose again
It's beauty in full bloom
Surrounded by a rainbow
Colors all abound
Music in the air
It's darkness will subside
Again I'll climb the rose
There is a serene seat
Waiting atop the petals
Deep inside my heart

My Foggy Trip across Long Island Sound

My destination awaits
I board the boat today
Traveling to my island haven
The air is quite humid
The reality of the fog is intense
I wonder, how can anyone see?
As we depart the mainland
A cool ocean breeze rolls in
I feel myself at ease
As the humidity departs
It's a peaceful trip
Water is calm as the boat
Caresses the ocean softly
The foghorn blares its alarm
But serenity holds my soul
As we travel through the sound
With this blinding mist in our path
I see the form of the island
Slightly through the white haze

It truly is a magical sight
As I watch the storm roll in
Swallowing the island in a dark fog
Clouds as pure as night
The sudden burst of rain and wind
Soaking as I took cover
In my shelter I see
The pure elements of nature
The wind
The water
Lightning and thunder
Encasing our reality in pure bliss
Raw emotion
I am afraid to close my eyes
Not even for a blink
In the worry of missing nature's gift
My soul is at peace
My heart is at rest
Forever etched into my mind

Through the Eyes of a Wolf

Sometimes I wish I could see
Through the eyes of a wolf
What images would there be

Would I travel in a pack
Or take the road alone
Which way will I attack

Will I feel the pride inside
As the wolf goes to hunt
With the loyalty resides

So majestic and so pure
The wolf, he speaks to me
To calm when I'm unsure

What instincts will become
As we do wander free
Our spirits turn into one

Where the Land Meets the Sea

Take me to the place
Where the land meets the sea
Watching the waves splash
Caressing the earth
Feeling simplicity

I feel the waves around
As I stand ankle deep
The wake of the water
Easing my every fear
Forgiving my soul's weep

I see the wind blowing
The grass moves with the breeze
The water ripples
It's such a peaceful sight
Brings a man to his knees

My conscious mind drifts
Away, out to sea
Calmly, the wind does dream
Slowly on the water
My soul floats with the breeze

I Can Smell the Sunrise

I can smell the sunrise
I hear the scents of roses
I see the wind on my skin
I feel the flavor of fruit
I taste the birds chirping

My goodness
I'm drunk again

The Dock

All alone on the dock
Two glasses and some whiskey
The night sky so clear
With all the stars to see

Reminiscing on our pasts
Giving voice to hopes and dreams
The ocean breeze reminds us
It's not always as it seems

Water splashing is the music
To sing and dance all night
As all our tears and laughter
Allow us such a sight

Time is lost with the wind
As we stare up at the sky
Wishing upon every star
Our thoughts can't be denied

Soon we see the sun rise
Breathtaking is the scene
Where did the hours all go
Time flew by unseen

We pour our last two glasses
The whiskey is on empty
Looking back on our night
Of this cherished memory

Pulling on the Strings of Fate

At night I watch the sky
I see the stars and moon
And I wonder to myself
Do you see this scene too?

Many nights I do wish
Upon the brightest star
With hopes the threads of fate
Will tell me where you are

Lonely are all the nights
Just wishing you were here
Teasing my desires
And stroking every fear

Laying my head to sleep
Morning brings a new day
Giving the string a pull
You know I'm on my way

Last Night I Dreamt

Last night I dreamt
I saw your eyes
Stare back at mine
Your smile
Brightened the room

Last night I dreamt
I felt your touch
On my skin
And your heartbeat
As I pulled you close

Last night I dreamt
I see your desire
Deep in your eyes
And felt the passion
Of your soft kiss

Last night I dreamt
Of you in my embrace
Your breath on my skin
Praying this moment
For time to stand still

The Devil in You

You have the devil in you, my dear
I can feel your flames from here
With a gaze my soul you sear
Your touch calms my every fear
But this pleasure seems so queer
As your voice invades my ear
With eyes closed you do appear
Timeless through all the year
As we find our souls cohere
Who is this puppeteer
With such a fantasy sincere
Upon this new frontier
No musing with but a tear

I Love You

Imagine our future lying in wait
Liquefying our time flows freely
On the shores to smooth the edge
Vividly, I see the ripples in the stream
Evenly the emotions move to caress
Your heart holds me close to you
Oh, the freedom of pure love
Unblemished through our trials ahead

Primal Desires

Feed our primal desires
If only for one night
Languidly caressing
As our hearts take flight

Each touch, each kiss
Fleeting is our time
I feel your craving gaze
This moment is our prime

This passion play before us
As each moment we pursue
Praying for no endings
As our devotion rings true

Holding My Heart

You are my sun

Melting the ice on the coldest days

You are my moon

Brightening the sky on the darkest night

You are my wind

I am left breathless everyday

Feel my kiss on your skin

As the breeze flows through

Desire builds within

Awaiting your touch…

Your kiss…

Trembling with anticipation

Close your eyes

Feel me within you

Dreaming of the moment

I am lost in your eyes

As you are lost in mine

Blue as the sky

Gems sparkling like stars

Holding my heart

Falling deeper in love

The silence of night

Speaking loudly between us

Miles apart

Yet only we know

Insanity driving wild

Only true lovers know

I Will Be Your Strength

I will be your strength when in need
I will be your eyes when you can't see
I will be the shoulder for your tears
I will be the heartbeat for your fears
I will be your voice when you can't talk
I will be your feet when you can't walk
I will carry you when you're too weak
For with this love is you I seek

My Siren, My Love

She teases me with her words
Conceiving these images pursued
Unsuppressed by the grasp of her hex
Misplaced is my discipline
Manipulated by my Siren
Unbridled greed brings me to my knees
With devotion to my empress
Snared by her mystical enchantment
My dominion lives within her grasp

Within the Eyes

Truth within

Feelings untold

Look deeper

Further is the key

Eyes hold meaning

Far more than words

They speak

Love

Honor

Pureness

Appearance holds

No value true

The words speak

Through deepest eyes

Thoughts from within

Does the heart bleed?

Is there sorrow?

Is there joy?

Questions answered fully

When you look

Deep into the eyes

The Storm

The water softly
Speaks but a whisper
Gathered along the shore
Until finally
The wind caresses
The ocean's body
Raging stronger
Forcefully
Passionately
As two become one
Within the midst
Of the heightened storm
The wind screams loudly
The ocean full to roar
Uncontrollably
Forcefully
The emotions of nature
Reaching its climax
Upon the furied waves
Both wind and water
Sharing the storm's bliss
Shouting through the clouds
Patiently waiting
For another moment
Of pure emotion
When the sun does pass

The Bonded Souls

The bond in essence
Is truly untamed
Unspoken through actions
Past…
Present…
Future…
What does truly hold the heart
Two souls as one
Through the darkness
Through the light
Past the sadness
Past the joy
The sacred bond
Only seen through clairvoyance
Through love
A gentle caress
Seeing through the looking glass
Into the eyes of your love
You don't see their eyes
You don't see reflection
You see…
Two hearts…
Two souls…
Bonded through matrimony
Yet words cannot describe…

Home within Your Embrace

Magic in your smile
Sparkle in your eyes
Bewitching is your voice
Melting with your touch
Bound to your soul
Strings of fate compelling
The moment endless
Swept by your gaze
Soften this lonely heart
Visions forthcoming
Fated to your side
Serenity eases fears
Parcae guarded the path
Home within your embrace

**Dedicated to AJ & Natalie for
always being my light in the darkness**

with

Thanks to Chris Brätt for helping
me get started on this adventure

and

To all my family and friends
for their encouragement and support.

To AJ, Daddy Loves You

I can still remember
The first moment I saw you
My life changed forever
How much I had no clue

I'm reminded every day
When I look into your eyes
I see the pain of your lows
And the joy of your highs

Watching you grow
All through the years
Makes me so proud
Your delight brings me tears

Your eyes so blue
Your smile just so bright
As I tuck you into bed
And give you a kiss goodnight

The love in your hugs
The freedom in your play
The pleasure in your singing
And dancing the night away

You sit on my lap
Or come lay next to me
I am dreading the day
When this will not be

But I know it true
This bond of ours
Father and son
Will travel so far

My pride and joy
My number one man
You are the world to me
I hope you understand

Tears may fall
The good with bad
All our ups and downs
I can never stay mad

Times you may cry
I can feel your pain
Please take my shoulder
I will keep you sane

To keep you safe
My best, I will do
One day you'll fly free
The finest life for you

My sweet, sweet boy
Daddy loves you so
You bring me such joy
How much you'll never know

My Sweet Natalie, Daddy Loves You

My sweet, sweet girl
So much strength to see
Watching you grow
Before my eyes I see

You are my peanut
Filled with so much joy
Such a little package
With a smile oh so coy

Smile lighting up the room
Shining sapphire eyes
So proud to see the life in you
Without a moment of despise

Dancing everywhere you can
All throughout the night
Spinning, dancing, singing
Just makes my heart take flight

The thrills of your happiness
Brings a smile I cannot hide
I wish to keep forever
My little angel by my side

Or chasing butterflies
As you run through the grass
As you hope this moment
Will forever last

And when you slide and swing
Gliding through the air
Your smile never leaving
As you play without a care

And when you hold my hand
Or kiss me on my nose
You always melt my heart
That's just how it goes

How strong is your will inside
Defiant as you may be
So proud to watch you grow
You are just so carefree

My sweet, sweet princess
Your resolve don't ever lose
Take my hand if you get lost
Allow me to help you choose

I'll carry you as you tire
So tightly in my arms
Wrap yourself around my neck
I'll keep you safe from harm

Daddy loves you, sweetie
Always my baby girl
Keep that music in your head
As you dance about the world

About the Author

Anthony Marcucio was born in Derby, Connecticut. He discovered a love for writing poetry in high school and has continued to cultivate that love to this day. Anthony currently works for a conservation organization which allows him to foster his love of nature while championing the cause to end the stigma associated with mental health. *Reflections of a Shattered Mind* is a journey through his life, from his battle with mental health to recovery, as well as finding love in his life.